Where is my daddy? He just answered the phone . We all know that look, soon he'll leave home. He'll take his boots and hooks when he goes. Someone lost power, if it goes quick he could be back in an hour?

The winds and ice caused the lines to drop. Lots of people lost power and there's no sign it'll stop.

I was on my way home, but we got one last call. So we head back out, it won't take long at all.

I won't be home just yet, because the roads are muddy and a little bit slick. I tried to stay on the road but the mud was too thick. Don't tell your mom I was driving the truck! I'll never hear the end of getting it stuck.

Looks like the Storm picked up through the night. There's a couple more homes without any lights. I'm off to work, love you goodnight.

Daddy where are you? I'm out of the states, I am in Haiti with a couple of mates. We are building power lines to villages that have never had lights. Soon a school just like yours for the first time will shine bright.

What is he
doing? No
bucket
trucks or
diggers, no
chainsaws
in sight.
Here we do
everything
by hand and
it takes all
of our
might.

He is
trimming
the lines
from a
coconut
tree. He
swings his
machete
to cut the
branches
free.

Surprise!
He
brought
fresh
coconuts
for all of
the guys.

Yes, we work as a team and we look out for each other. No, they are not all your uncles. I just call them my brothers.

These guys on the pole are always watching my back. Yes, I will thank them. I'm sure they will love that.

Today I woke up not a cloud in the sky, the winds have died down so I'm climbing up high. What are you doing? How was your day? Did you finish your chores so you could go play?

Tell your mother I love her. I know she is doing it all. Don't give her any trouble while I'm out on a call.

We are getting real close to coming back home. Just a couple more climbs up a couple more poles.

As I look down below I feel nothing but pride when I see the smiling faces of people that pass by.

Daddy where are you? Hey kids up I'm up in the sky, riding in my buggy on energized lines. No, I can't feel it. I wear a special suit that makes the power go over me and under my boots . So do all your chores and be good for your mama. I'll call you from the hotel don't cause any drama.

We don't just climb wooden poles, we also climb steel towers. The view is amazing I could stay here for hours.

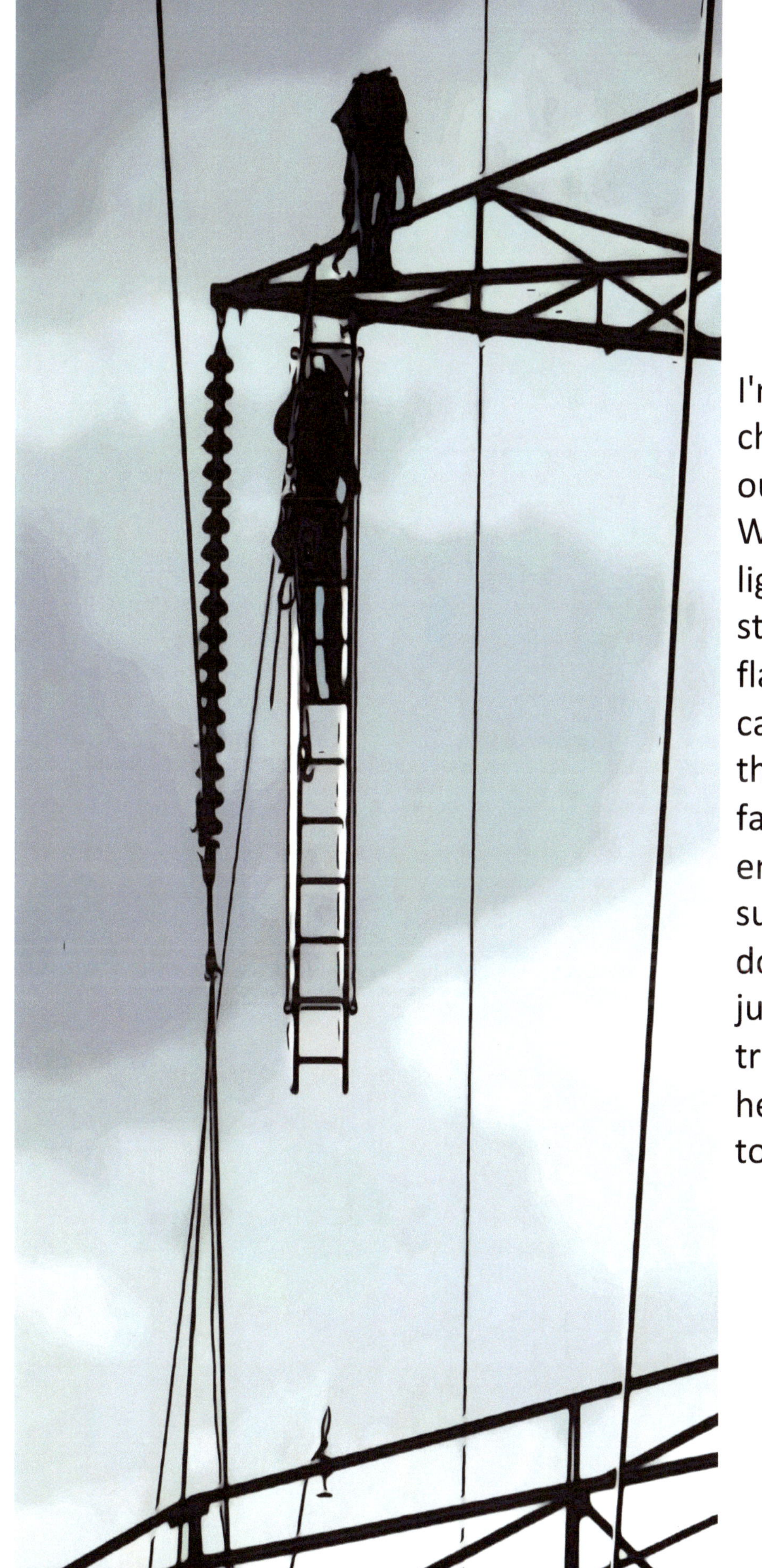

Yes, its a little like a circus on our flying trapeze but we have lots of safety to put your little minds at ease. What am I doing?
I'm changing out bells. When lightening strikes it flashes and causes them to fail. Soon enough the sun will go down, I'll jump in my truck and head back to town.

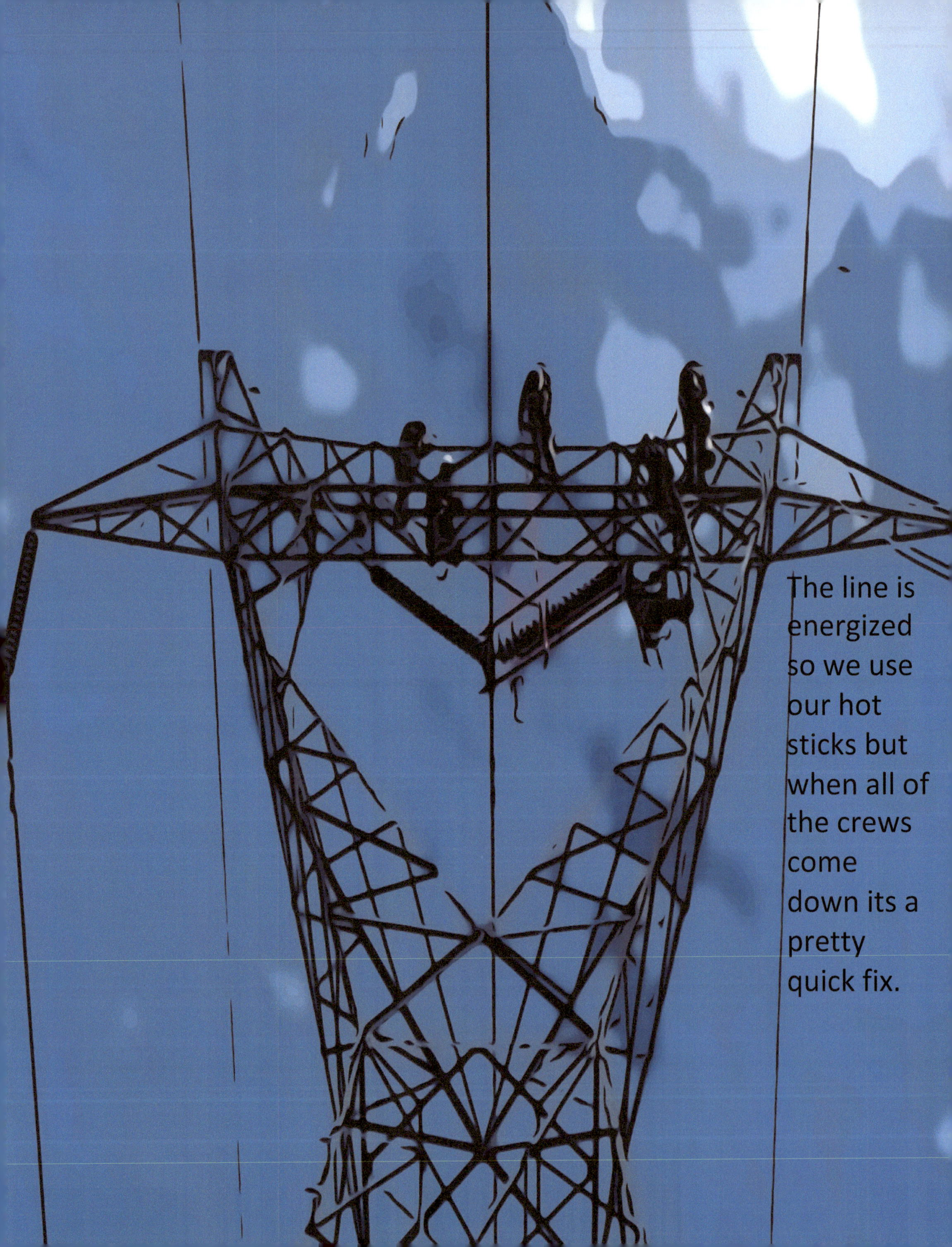
The line is
energized
so we use
our hot
sticks but
when all of
the crews
come
down its a
pretty
quick fix.

How tall is that truck? Well it goes pretty high, 185 feet straight up in the sky.

Today, we are practicing safety. Remember that buggy I was in a couple days ago? This is what we do if the cart won't go. We clip a rope on the wire and hook it to our chest. Then get out of the buggy and let gravity do the rest.

Hey there kiddo, I can see you down there! We fly in planes patrolling the lines, that we have to maintain.

Daddy where are you ? I had to leave town. It's been a long day running rope from the ground. We always take turns like everyone should do. It makes the day a little easier for you and your crew.

How is the dog doing? Give him a big pat on the head, then brush up those teeth and crawl into bed. I'll call you tomorrow so answer the phone. Before you all know it, daddy will be home.

Look at this Kids, its quite the
machine. I think you are right it could
climb anything. This track bucket truck
can go off the road it won't get stuck
and can carry a heavy load.

Hurricane Sandy caused a lot of destruction. It left NYC under construction. We won't stop until every home has power. We'll work all day and into the night hour.

Where am I sleeping? I am on nice cot, there are hundreds of lineman and it gets really hot. We all worked hard but we don't smell that pretty. Tonight we'll sleep tight here in Tent City.

We just finished up, I should be home by end of the day. We are just saying goodbye to some friends we met along the way.

Life as a
lineman is
rewarding
and fun but
the feeling
of home
cannot be
outdone.

www.ingramcontent.com/pod-product-compliance
Lightning Source LLC
Chambersburg PA
CBHW042020110726
48006CB00004B/1159